To Every Thing...

poems of seasons,

nature, and life

by: Jenifer Loggins

cover photo by Madi Loggins

for

you

may you

find beauty

and growth

in yourself

in every season

Live in each season as it passes;

breathe the air,

drink the drink,

taste the fruit,

and resign yourself

to influence the earth.

-Henry David Thoreau

Wishes

When my hands gripped sand

as a little child,

I watched how fluidly it left me

despite the fury of my grasp.

How it'd whistle away with whispers of August,

leaving wishes in its stead

-in my head

not my hands

to scatter like grains.

But holding on to wishes, even tightly,

doesn't always make them stay

and maybe,

sometimes

it's better off that way.

To every thing there is a season,

and a time to every purpose under the heaven:

Ecclesiastes 3: 1-8

Winter

I gave up trembling.

What enamored me mostly,

were stories to tell.

What Summer Failed to Praise

Bone colored skin

silhouettes the backdrop of winter.

Stark radiance amongst pine

and gnarly underbrush.

I'll never captivate an audience,

poise and style of a ballerina in arabesque

delicate arms saying come hither

mighty oaks sway and bow…

Oh sycamore,

how the bleak of winter

  illuminates

what summer failed to praise.

January

When January skies turned punishing,

 she's a ghost's cape sallowed

from aged bitterness;

how she bantered with rivers of blackbirds,

how they shape shifted

across the gibbous last evening

erasing winter's rainbow of color,

whiting out what is left of our sky…

I'll tuck my painful bones inside

-I can't fly away like those geese did,

can't form my body into acute angles

and follow where the blackbirds went

when they buried the treasures of December

and all of his bewitching sunset.

While I Sleep

I drove myself through the night,

dampened shadows canopied the road

like some nightmare.

Tunneling me, lashing out.

I feel reckless,

out of control

and unrestrained.

I feel catapulted

in my most vulnerable of states.

Broken stars of glass

echo my screaming, as they stand by watching

as I lie

free

falling

to wolves and wilderness while I sleep.

Obscurity

I need to go back to obscurity,

lime lights never did much for me,

watch the world go by through the roses

-my secret garden I built it for...

Hide my soul away, tucked in the corner

like a bird in the box;

let me trickle out

like the Geminids I could never find.

A shooting star of flashing moments,

if only in my mind.

Dislocated

I feel

out of place

in my own body:

displaced, fractured.

No place I belong

or can fit myself into.

An outsider.

No body can relate to mine,

-my curves,

what encompasses me,

-my volume,

my viscosity;

no one knows,

or wants to understand.

I'm alone in foreign land

that I call my home.

While grasping for connection,

thirsting for what I can't have yet,

steeping in a water

a place that's not

my own.

What the Bluebirds Knew

Frozen fog throws blankets

around my survival,

while frost laden tree limbs

beckon me to embrace

the intricate etching it's left on the red maple,

and my bewildered mind.

How I don't care for once

how the cold is biting,

how my fingers flaming red

symbolize my soul set on to burning.

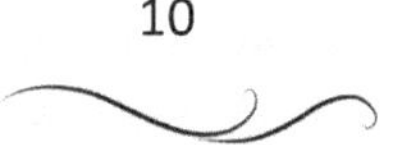

How I've slept through winter before like a bear,

but just now, I've come alive.

Like the bluebirds flocking merrily

in her silence,

they knew it

how death is resurrection-

and the ability to revive your soul

within frost's clutches,

is as spellbinding as this morning and all her majesties.

Dreaming Tree

Dreaming tree casts supernal,

halo orbits the moon…

her subconscious eternal

and daylight comes too soon…

She etches the velvet,

the cloud-stricken sky.

Bone fingers regretting,

twisting time as she cries…

But he'll blanket her, swoon her,

phosphorescence of light.

He'll strum at her heartstrings,

'til broad morning light

and he'll leave her with only,

his angelic mark-

how his halo of lightness,

broke her deepest dark.

Reverie

In my sheets

a cool daydream,

my body will hollow out a warm space.

It's a comfort,

heat is,

after feeling chilled.

Feeling that shocking polarity,

lets me recognize warmth for what it is.

I bed down.

These bundled sheets

are my reverie…

My day was long

but no more,

I'll soar,

for my dreams

are just

within reach.

Snow

If you want to take a walk in the snow,

go write a poem,

open the doors

 to that part of you where it's cold.

An intentional cellar of a place

 best left closed and unspoken.

Where whisps of nothingness

once kissed your cheeks and nose like Judas'

 betrayal. But welcome you back now

to brisk and haunting land

that never froze you-

never killed you-

and now it's made you most alive,

the kindest warmth of a thawing bleeding heart.

Ok

The sky is cobalt,

yellow bells showing out,

outside,

my window-

my cold-

 is not yet a reflection of it.

Life goes on without me to warm it,

ice in my heart will thaw again, soon.

Like when frost creeps in

and kisses my garden

-I'm wrapped in cold,

this moment.

But there's beauty in those seconds

where you don't feel ok,

but you know

you're going to be…

Spring

I long for fresh dirt

my fingers encircling,

grasping new bulbs. Growth.

Dawning

Born from complacence

and womb of darkened night,

your beams are pulsing vitality

a glorious birth of a new morning

flooding my eyes-

a sort of radiant vision.

I'm seeing through those rose -colored glasses,

each day is a celebration,

from hopping chickadees throat

and mockingbirds' jealous beak.

Mindfulness

There's something to be told about the morning.

The sun

 has not yet made its arrival,

birds

huddled hushedly in their nests.

The doe,

still and statuesque against the fog

gazes almost ghostlike into the wood line.

No passersby or gentle hum of motors.

Only the promising silence-

the gentle murmurs

of mindfulness.

Circles

Black birds seem to transfigure.

Each raindrop that hits wet pavement

are tiny infinite circles reaching up and out,

then melding into its brother.

Incessant birdsong from a harbor

in the sweetgum,

how they seem to gleefully admire the shower,

how their hope for quenching

has come to be.

Praising Him with tiny beaks,

tiny joyous hearts.

-Infinite circles

of praises

and the abundant showering they receive.

Seasons

Sometimes words aren't needed,

for some to hear what you have to say…

I saw the dogwood petal

in the shape of a cross. The crown

gloriously embedded within its head,

within my heart.

Saw how she quilted for you,

unknowing

of the piece of her heart

she would leave you

in that fabric,

green, floral and lovely.

Like spring and the awakening,

the way we are loved

without hearing any word

other than birdsong.

And seeing

the much deeper meaning,

in every season He sends.

Jonquils in the Breeze

You lined acorns

horizontally on the picnic table

"For the squirrels" you'd say

"so they won't even have to look for them"

Your heart is just the sweetest,

and mine, I feel, may melt.

As I watch the springtime sun shimmer

on what's golden in my life,

watch the zephyr shuffle your hair

as you crouch by that tree,

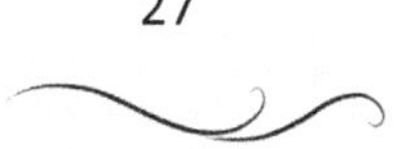

watch

how perfectly my life is unfolding

-like jonquils in the breeze.

Safe

Am I in control of something

that's completely out of mine?

Days like these my nerves are a fraying

thread. Irritated and unstable-

like our atmosphere,

the way she punishes.

Her black skies that loom vengefully,

wind ravaging and angry,

the eerie whistle it makes from my sunroom

is a spilling of secrets

of a wrath that is yet to come.

I wait for it,

I can feel it, unsettling,

unnerving.

No one can control this weather-

we just brace ourselves

while it's calm.

Plant ourselves firmly

in that safe spot

and be ready

for the furies

that will affect

someone

-but this time

Is it going to be

Me?

Ceraunophilia

Your echo rumbled across my night's sky,

shook my house,

found me,

no longer quaking...

but lit me up

in a state of wonderment.

One flash, sparked into two,

rolled over my valleys

that once stood

watered in fear.

Now find me not,

down in stormy furrows,

while my bells writhe beneath your zeal,

but cloaked in covers,

in a feeling

of harmlessness and utmost awe.

Wildflowers

If you'll be the rain,

I'll be the sun.

We'll plant seeds together.

Dig this small hole,

hug them with dirt,

tuck each one in gently,

kiss each forehead with misty goodnights,

patiently waiting tiny tendrils

emerging bashfully

rubbing their eyes to find their place

among the wildflowers of all kinds.

35

How they coexist in the meadow

so colorfully, each like you and me

-with differences

so much that really,

we are the same.

Homesickness

The way the screen door slammed

in exuberance

my small legs carried me like wind,

like water

to you. Toward the windchimes

that tangled on the breeze.

The dandelion haze of impending summer

and the wafting of laundry tumbling,

diffusing sunshine with that homely

fragrance.

I ran to you across that meadow,

followed my heart that was partly yours...

followed my longing

my deepest source of safety

'til daylight vanished.

Leaving an era igniting brighter

than the soft yellow hum

of summers across the field

and the dandelions of May

in my mind.

Summer

Splashes, golden sun,

picturesque days, and the stars-

punctured velvet nights.

So Much More Than Easy

Somehow, I feel I've known you before…

Reading your words,

maybe strange, the familiarities

I recall as I read them.

Scratchy dollar store lounge chairs

in a circle

-a congregation circumferenced around

Mawmaw's metal dish pan in the center

we'd talk,

we'd toss

and I was so small,

but those days felt so much bigger.

Plucking silken strands

from silver queens,

tossing their minty robes

to rest in the pan.

Like my memories

that rested way back,

seemingly withered like old corn silks,

'til sweet nostalgic poetry

plucks them out of me,

tosses

me back

to when days were long,

and so much more than easy.

July

I stood there that summer,

heat radiating coruscating waves

off the hood of my car.

Gathered my belongings

that never did belong-

one quick stride, and slight of hand.

Dust to dust as July's rain rolled in

settling it finally, after so long

leaving the ashes to soak;

and finding rest at last

in wherever they may fall.

Stories

I rode the wave;

was mine, and no one else's

I stayed in the shallows

where my eyes couldn't deceive me

so long...

I saw fish swim 'round my ankles.

We are the same,

my life no greater than his life-or hers.

I rocked each toiling wave

and I swallowed sand along the way

was pushed to the dreaded place
of "out of my comfort"

to find I could no longer see
what was swimming below,

what tugged at me
what threatened.

I climbed up on those angry waters
of waves that challenged me

and found my place back on the sand.
My story

-no one else's-

No longer to sink
or be tattered.

No longer clinging to fear

or angst of being reckoned.

Rose Petals

Our eyes blossomed

with the longing of rose petals.

Faintest pink,

brush of a kiss

is your smile-

curling up

to show me glimpses of sunlight.

Little ladies

dance around your arm,

dew drops bead your brow

as you rocked them.

You held my gaze,

broke my sepia sunrise,

painted my skies

in pink passion.

Trailing my world,

with brushstrokes of fondness

and the loveliest

admiration

when your petals

fell to rest at my feet.

Metaphors

when you walk outside,

catch glimpse of the sky,

re-view your world

to see poetic metaphors...

see not the clouds-

but a field of cornflowers.

ethereal angels dancing-

billows of ballerinas

tiptoeing across the sun.

gossamer wings fanned out

as he blushes aglow,

peach in his cheeks

-so vibrant, but meek.

while we all lie here,

and marvel

from seeing the abstract visions

of what some can't seem to see.

Under the Streetlamps

and the Moon

I remember the time

the rocking chairs grew tiring,

the street lamps of the alley

vibed an inviting glow.

Cabernet in our veins

and the moon's crazy dare,

I guess we just felt the need to move…

I still hear the crunch of gravel in the midnight,

lost in the moment

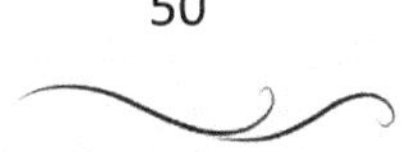

as we belted "The Civil Wars"

along the hills of 5th avenue.

How time seemed to entrance us,

we watched each body in the trees flicker,

resonating with the dream like state

we were in that moment,

the fireflies and all their enthusiasm

that warm July night under the stars.

We walked across town

like we hadn't a care

young and fun,

unblemished from the pain of the world then.

I'd go back if that tree were still standing,

I think we could create that halcyon again.

I'll listen for your laughter reach my ears

and in that moment,

in that second

when our souls caught fire with freedom,

under the street lights

 and the moon...

Harbor

You keep coming back here

looking for a place to land,

for shelter.

I see you,

how your boat

thrashes in the harbor,

your harbor,

where anger, bitterness, and resentment

toss you

creeps up 'til your head is held under,

and negativity

swallows you up.

Reach for my hand. I'll try to pull you out

again

and

again.

You're getting heavy though with all that resentment
drowning you...

Let it go.

Let it ripple away

by the water.

Don't let your harbor of what is heavy drown you

again,

and again,

and again.

Seas of our sky

I'm thinking aloud

how the sky looks right now…

how it's an ocean turned upside down

see its waves?

Its variations of blues and grays?

How it eddys and twirls?

The pearly foam adorning

each tip of its bubble,

of how flocks of birds

weaving over white oaks,

are really schools of fishes,

darting through wriggling corals.

Swimming,

soaring, the seas of our sky.

Gravity

The way water has no control over itself

is this humbling feeling...

Black waves towering

boiling over,

levitating its body

over the rest of its sea,

by some command,

by what power?

I see the gentle way you love me.

Like the ocean

and its waves tripping over itself,

crashing

 into each other

by no commands.

With such astounding power

that it's terrifying.

Something so raging and dynamic

but with easiness,

the involuntary gravitational power

on love and billowing waves.

Coronal

We trudged for miles while the sun boiled us,

sweat beading our pores

seething salt to the dirt road we tread on.

We were golden then

our differences of age,

the honeycomb haze

and summer.

The bees fixed on our chests

calm and un-hasty

we wore them like armor

-like a ribcage of gold.

Where had we walked from?

I still can't say…

Those miles of dirt between us all

we knew who we were then,

stood tall, empowered…

Now I can see it was all facets of myself,

the way we all hold different sides,

like puzzle pieces trying to fit a mold,

like diamonds

 cut in the most exquisite of ways,

like our journey and where we came from

and coronal days of summer

as daughters of the King.

Autumn

Like the autumn fire

that taught her, dazzling colors

lie within- waiting…

September's Sovereign

Your long dark curls

glint auburn in sunsets,

natural fire woven in your crown

to mark your royalty.

I've told you, my darling,

you- are everything!

That beautiful smile and old soul,

exquisite porcelain skin

like some doll with delicate fragility.

Sweeping tendrils.

Tender of heart-

heart of a fairy princess,

with enough strength

to fight any battle,

but with the empathy

to grace the calm.

Abditory

It's fall in my head,

golden afternoon day.

I walk through the forest,

the fields and the hay-

are gleaming and sparking

by light of the sun.

Red tails swirl high up,

screeching,

their hunt isn't done.

The creek babbles gently

her lusts and repairs;

telling the catbirds

all the world's cares.

Welcomes me home

by the beech tree's wave,

her trunk bent, just so,

is my seat that she's saved.

And the crushed velvet mosses

carpet my toes underfoot,

caressing my skin

and my worries are put

in the water to wash

all of my cares away

in my soul's abditory

this delightful fall day.

The Greatest

Freckles smattered

 across your cheeks and nose.

Is anything ever cuter,

than the way your eyes-

big, blue, and beautiful

light up when you giggle

so mischievously?

Like I should keep my eye on you, a little more so-

but in the rest of my years living

-I can't think of anything better.

That of a Lamb

Write what's in your heart,

says Wordsworth and his poetry...

take "my heart's breathings

and fill it out onto paper."

He knew the way it'd fill my heart,

flood my mind

each moment...

I need an escape,

that ink on paper

is the sister I never had.

When my words are misconstrued

she understands it,

when my courage

to stand in a crowd is syncopal,

she is my words,

my eloquence.

Never leave me.

Continue to be the breath

in the alveoli of my lungs,

continue to bleed yourself

onto these cream sheets.

They can't stay in there forever,

bubbling in my heart

on the verge of eruption.

-My voice is that of a lamb

seeking to be a lion-

hoping for an escape out of turmoil,

for a ray of light amidst the dark.

Un-Nocturnal

I find myself

treasuring the moon

sometimes

mesmerized

by her essence.

I want

so much

more,

this need

to shine a light

through someone's

darkness.

So many

are still sleeping,

and I myself

have been

 the one;

to toss

and turn

in sheets on end

-un-nocturnal.

Neglecting

all her worthiness,

to give

 all praises

 to the sun.

Black Dog

I wrapped the crocheted blanket

around my shoulders a little more tightly

as moonbeams crawled

across my kitchen floor.

I saw shadows,

 how the grass bowed to encroaching winds,

heard the howling

echo in the space across the field.

I looked for you to find I was alone,

the dappled clouds rolled over the moon and I shivered

-like this feeling of cold and fear crept over my body

The way the clouds did

as they diminished her pearlescent presence.

The black dog in the distance

joined the field grass harmony of howling

-my fear.

A warning to me to be on the lookout

creeping closer to my backdoor

and too close for comfort at the time.

How many times

has fear found me alone and trembling?

Alerting me,

cautioning voice,

something I once thought was ominous

I see now, a symbolic friend.

I keep searching for someone

to guard me in dark-fall

but there's power in me that howls against all danger.

Fear is no longer enemy to me,

but intuition

and it's always been bellowing,

as some roar within myself.

To Kill

I took you

in my hands

small and trembling.

I wrapped you

with ribbons

of red,

the color

of my adrenaline

-my blood that pumped through erratically.

I took you

to the garden,

my morning sun that shined

for me again today.

Eyes waking up

to behold the brilliance,

like mine have.

Soft fall winds

erupt

 my ivory skin

in compounded chills.

I took you.

Laid your four walls

in the hole I dug for myself, long ago,

irrationally,

fully ready to immerse…

I saw you,

the way you'd box me in

so comfortably.

Burying myself alive

-when there was more I had to give

first.

I took you,

my sweet little box of fear.

Fearfully,

somewhat regrettably,

uncomfortably,

I took you,

I bury you,

I put you to rest now with winter.

To slowly unravel

that ribbon

That's connectively tying me

into paralyzing knots

Suspended

Once I found myself standing near the edge,

sedimentary rock holding the weight of my body

never wavered.

Thoughts of falling never crossed me

-my boots anchored to that ancient rock.

I muse over flying.

Like the dream I had

I hang-glided over Straight Mountain…

Suspended

so elevated,

so free

I didn't want to come down to those calling me below,

to the speckled doe,

and her fawn in the clearing,

to the glare of the tears of the pine.

I loved that freedom, that solace,

how things look

 up here.

How it whispered in my ears,

tickled my neckline,

caressed my fleeing body, like a lover in the night.

But I'm suspended now in reality,

I'll fathom the days

soaring isn't impressive to me anymore,

billowing over what lies beyond

someone's greener pasture.

I'll stand here like beech trees

their bashful pinks

I sometimes catch sight of in forests.

I'll be like them-

Blushing from who I am,

where wind planted me,

and that I've kept my colors in spite of

the world

and some ghastly gray.

the fall

wild fire of colors,

oh it's now, the time has come

burn on out, and go to sleep

-we'll see what you become

"The trees know about the winter.

About the change. About the falling.

About the loss. And they grow anyway..."

-Erin Van Vuren

Life Seasons

As for life seasons,

find beauty in change, just so…

Seasons come- but, go.

I can feel it moving me

as if swaying with the wind,

this sense of change,

I cannot explain

-the seasons turn again.

So many years I couldn't tell,

but I've become in line

-not only do leaves change color,

so do seasons of the mind...

Silver

I'd like to say I've earned you,

tiny little silver.

Tiny tinsel birthed

from where wisdom was conceived.

I gave them to my mother

-she gave them to hers...

No one see you yet

just me-

a lucky talisman of things I've weathered

my silver lining, hiding in the dark place

underneath

only visible if I put myself out there

put it on display

for the light to glint my secret

a treasure baring its own ray.

Birth

A laugh, a tear, an exasperated sigh,

these are all born from something greater.

Me, born from my mother;

tornado sirens blaring, synchronizing her cries

the pain,

the blood given up.

But to live through that pain,

and still be in love with the product,

is so much more than we could fathom,

or even be humanly capable to.

Because it is bigger, it is spiritual,

it is wrenchingly powerful.

Those things we give life to,

the things we nurture, to live.

Do we grow love?

Generate forgiveness, or empathy?

Or give life to hatefulness or resentment?

Will we be proud of what we've given birth to?

Will we look back with longing

to the times of our lives

and be pleased

with what we have created?

In every painful life event we've suffered,

will we choose to love the fruits of it?

Or curse the pain that delivered us here

where we now stand?

There have been many afflictions

that make or break a life, and not always fair...

but I see that to understand growth

and forgiveness

you must first be reborn

from some overwhelming pain.

Autoimmune

When the life feels sucked out

of me like tiny holes

piercing

watch my life flow out,

all of my energy.

I'm faded now

but you can't tell?

I wear it,

and sometimes

-I wear it well.

No energy.

I lift my arms in failure.

I rest my eyes but feel the same-

Guiltiness.

That restlessness that drifts in filling

where my livelihood should be

Where it

USED

 to be.

And I breathe,

it'll come back to me.

NOT

 gonna lay down here

because I'm not dying

not today,

I will decide it.

Was Taken

I'm finding now, the truth of it.

That time, in no certain number,

no set amount of years or days,

helped bind the wound of your loss.

What seemed unbearable,

what intruded every thought I had,

day,

night.

It's eased with the bandage of time.

The tears I'd let fall freely,

each time you crossed my mind;

collected

as a well in my heart

that now treasures every memory,

but without absolute grief.

And now I feel joy

when I wear the sunflowered apron,

the color of lapis

and sunny as your smile.

And with the melodies I sing in the kitchen

the way you did

with the cooking and the cleaning.

When the first jonquil of spring

lifts her beautiful face to the sun;

I'll exclaim my excitement.

 You are with me

in the scent of the gardenia, or lilac

or when I read my children

 a story from our book.

You didn't leave me. I now know.

You just chose to dwell in my heart,

so your essence could live on,

in me,

through time.

It's what you gave me,

not

what I once thought was taken.

Transplant Shock

I dug up the peony bush

growing careless in the hayfield

-no one to nurture it

since my grandfather

passed on to Heaven.

I loved it, wanted it, so badly…

If not for its beauty

-but a reminder of what I'd lost.

How he planted them there for nothing more

than to put a smile on my grandma's face

when he'd grace her with their elegant

colossal blossoms.

Sarah Bernhardt in pink,

 proud and lovely,

and strong.

I didn't notice then

it needed not,

for me to take it home, to nurture it.

She was holding her head up

Just fine on her own...

I planted this beauty

 in my own backyard of selfishness.

Each day how she'd wither and furl.

I'm learning now how the peony felt,

ripped from grounds

she'd established herself into

roots shorn

severed.

How I feel now

that my roots are being threatened

A peony in transplant shock.

Scalded

My hand was scalded

when I reached it under the water

-my own mistake

for not checking it first.

Temperature burning me

leaving my skin reeling,

confused...

I've made this mistake

 in other ways.

Disoriented from the sting

of jumping into something,

both feet-

immersed in it.

Yeah, I feel it

the undesired pain

of impulsive decisions.

I'll ice it-

I'm sure it's going to heal.

So go ahead

leave your mark

 on me.

Tiny Grasps

I'm happy.

That star still fizzles in my right hand.

I could never reach, I thought

-would always be unattainable to me-

So small and humble,

Uneducated.

I could never be as valiant,

as to pluck one from the heavens too;

surely,

I'd fall if I ever did reach…

And that-

was called losing.

Maybe I will,

still?

But still,

I'll hold it tighter,

as winning

still shines

even in tiny grasps.

Hate and Love

part I

Vulnerable

How you stripped me,

bare skinned

of good thoughts,

small wishes,

self- respect.

That's called vulnerable you know?

Where you hit me-

a shotgun shell

blown through

my walls of confidence

-some holey protection I have now.

and that was the first time,

I'd ever

held that gun.

--------stop destroying your own self esteem----------------

part II

Face

You tell me lies sometimes

and I've believed you

before…

I see through your transparency,

each time you've tried to put me down,

made me doubt,

made me question.

I've never

liked a liar.

Especially,

the one that shares the same face I do.

-------------Stop putting down the face in the mirror-----------

part III

Yourself

Is there any better truth

than to love others

you must first love yourself?

In the end

she's all we will have of anything tangible.

Be kind to her face in the mirror,

for who else really knows

her heart?

 Her mind? Her spirit?

That body,

The one,

 you sometimes are unkind to.

The one,

you've judged too harshly.

The one,

that puts her life into others'

-pours her life

into the lives

of others-

She is lovely,

and powerful,

and worthy of your respect.

So tell me,

how any other love can be capable,

if that one

extraordinary heart

isn't nurtured first?

---------------YOU are always worthy, just know it-------------

Part IV

Not / It / Me

In my skin I've trembled here

pale, and elastic.

An article to house Me

-but Not, define Me.

I am Not, It

-my skin is Not Me,

but yet, It

 is mine.

I have filled

 Its spaces

with invisible growth.

I have filled It,

and am bursting out.

Expulsion of seams

that can still stretch,

still burgeon

-with Me.

----There is always room to grow and redefine ourselves----

From the Ground

Dark stains.

It's what seeps into fabric the deepest
to leave a blighted mark.

It's not lore,
but history-
the kind we don't want repeating itself.

That Sunday, but so many more...
That lack of love,
empathy, and understanding
screams from the ground.

That stain won't leave,

but we will grow from it,

rise from our earth

like OUR history will.

A reminder,

of times we don't want repeated.

Peace and War

Some words

 pierce daggers into my heart,

that organ

bejeweled in my chest.

It thrives from peace,

though in the midst of a war…

My blood

will pump fluidly throughout it,

steady

and warm, involuntary.

These precarious times we fight for

invade our calm,

falter within us

like asymmetrical stones.

To gather them?

To set them away?

Can there be balance?

When isn't our entire life some epic battle,

between daggers,

 and peace, and war?

Forgiveness

You took what's heavy from me

-I didn't realize I was carrying

so much.

Didn't see how tired I was under all

that weight.

You took my eyes and gave them

clarity.

I won't lie- It was really hard to see you...

Clouded judgement,

so easy to boil underneath my own

wrath and shortcomings.

I was blinded,

you helped me see.

I was cynical,

you helped me believe,

shrouded me in white linen,

covered my bruised blue lips,

kissed

those wounds there

I helped give to myself.

You wiped me

clean.

You gave me

light.

You're something so incredibly hard,

yet so easy to accept

-that by punishing you,

I only punish

 myself...

Fireproof

Maybe,

I am "fireproof"

Except, only everything

breaks my heart...

His pain, hers,

I keep your secrets-

They burn me

like my own little fires.

But see, it's tempered then,

my heart is

-and my temper's been a hot one-

but through heat,

is where resilience hardens.

(inspired from The National "Fireproof")

Lines

I think about life-

these lines…

a descendance from some-

that I'm not entirely sure of.

My birth.

How three connected me

to the world of my mother's womb,

to her life.

That strong line

that gave me mine…

the delicate etchings,

tender beginnings

of lines

 of their own.

Mapping out the space

round my eyes

where tears have seeped

or laughter has crinkled,

where weariness

once plumed.

The places,

my body has been forgiving to stretch,

or maybe-to shrink back down.

What I've felt ashamed for-

Those stripes, I tell myself,

have been earned,

as my right.

A branding, to remind me

what a woman's body can do.

The faint blue lines

peeking pallid undertones,

under my skin,

reminding me,

just how alive I really am-

Blood lines,

veining art

gifting me life,

sprouting my existence.

How I'll try walking the straight one,

but pick myself up

from the shoulders of life's bends,

more tries, more times

than I can count on.

Heart lines

grasping outward

like some magnetic

pulling force

to those kindred of spirits

with most invisible bonds.

The connections we make,

the lines of our journey,

the lines of the pages

to the books our lives leave published.

From the doorway of this life,

to move on to the next.

I've seen the green lines of the monitor

as they wave,

watched them wane lower,

as the heart releases for its last time.

Moments like this

I ponder life as a complex wonder,

And that instant

when the doorway of physical life is closed

-overwhelming and spiritual

to watch the let go

of physical existence

to the realm of the spiritual life line....

Dance

I belong out here

wild and unbridled

to dance with her water

when she wants to carry me.

To fall to my knees

if she bears down.

To open wide irises, green and yearning,

to her sky and conveying crown.

About the Author

Jenifer Loggins is a small- town poet, mother, wife, and registered nurse and avid lover of nature. Author of her first published collection of poetry "To Have Learned" and her second collection, newly released "To Every Thing…"

As a woman, Jenifer is proud to use her voice through poetry to reach into the hearts and souls of another, to help the reader find empowerment, healing, and growth within themselves. She wants her readers to see that there is beauty in every 'season' of life. She sees it everywhere, in every thing.

To every thing there is a season,

and a time to every purpose under the heaven:

A time to be born, and a time to die;

A time to plant, and a time to pluck up that which is planted;

A time to kill, and a time to heal;

A time to break down, and a time to build up;

A time to weep, and a time to laugh;

A time to mourn, and a time to dance;

A time to cast away stones, and a time to gather stones together;

A time to embrace, and a time to refrain from embracing;

A time to get, and a time to lose;

A time to keep, and a time to cast away;

A time to rend, and a time to sew;

A time to keep silence, and a time to speak;

A time to love, and a time to hate;

A time of war, and a time of peace.

Ecclesiastes 3:1-8